W9-DFV-933

21st
Century
Junior
Library

WORKING AT A SCHOOL

by Katie Marsico

CHERRY LAKE PUBLISHING * ANN ARBOR, MICHIGAN

CHERRY LAKE
Publishing

Published in the United States of America by Cherry Lake Publishing
Ann Arbor, Michigan
www.cherrylakepublishing.com

Content Adviser: Sharon Castle, PhD, Associate Professor of Elementary Social Studies, George Mason University, Fairfax, Virginia
Reading Consultant: Cecilia Minden-Cupp, PhD, Literacy Specialist and Author

Photo Credits: Cover and page 4, ©iStockphoto.com/RonTech2000; page 6, ©PhotoCreate, used under license from Shutterstock, Inc.; page 8, ©iStockphoto.com/jashlock; cover and pages 10 and 12, ©iStockphoto.com/bonniej; page 14, ©Sally and Richard Greenhill/Alamy; page 16, ©Jeff Greenberg/Alamy; cover and page 28, ©sonya etchison, used under license from Shutterstock, Inc.; cover and page 20, ©Flashon Studio, used under license from Shutterstock, Inc.

LIBRARY OF CONGRESS CATALOGING-IN-PUBLICATION DATA
Marsico, Katie, 1980–
  Working at a school / by Katie Marsico.
      p. cm.
  Includes index.
  ISBN-13: 978-1-60279-266-1
  ISBN-10: 1-60279-266-6
  1. School employees—Juvenile literature. I. Title.
  LB2831.5.M37 2009
  372.12'01—dc22   2008004764

*Cherry Lake Publishing would like to acknowledge the work of
The Partnership for 21st Century Skills.
Please visit* www.21stcenturyskills.org *for more information.*

CONTENTS

Teachers are happy when their students are learning.

What Is a School?

A bell rings! It is time for classes to begin. All the boys and girls hurry to their classrooms. Bells help to keep everyone on time for classes.

A **principal**, **teachers**, and other people work in schools. Schools give boys and girls a place to explore many things. All of the workers at the school help students learn.

Reading is one of the most important skills you learn in school.

You probably learned how to read at school. Now you can read this book! What do you like best about school? Many people do different jobs in schools. They all work together to make school a great place to learn. Let's take a look at some school workers.

Safety is an important part of any science project.

School Workers

Teachers help students learn to read and count. They help students learn about science and history. Gym teachers show students how to exercise. Music teachers help kids learn to sing. Art teachers show students how to draw.

Teachers plan learning activities for students. Sometimes they give students **assignments** to take home.

A teacher explains an assignment to her students.

Those assignments are called homework. Sometimes teachers give students tests. All of these things help teachers know if students are learning.

The principal of a school keeps track of everything at the school. She makes sure students are safe and ready to learn.

Look!

Teachers and other school workers use many things to help kids learn. Look around the next time you are in your classroom. Can you name five objects that help you learn? Hint: Pencils and books are two examples.

The principal and teachers meet often. They work together to make sure students are learning.

She also makes sure that everyone follows the school rules.

The **secretary** helps the principal keep the school organized. He often takes care of letters and e-mails. The secretary answers the phone. He helps parents with their questions.

The **librarian** helps teachers and students find the facts they need. He can help you find just the right book to read.

Cafeteria workers make sure students have a healthy lunch.

Whose job is it to take care of students who get sick or hurt at school? This is the job of the school nurse. Sometimes a student is too sick to stay in class. Then the school nurse sends the student home.

Many other school workers also do their part to keep students safe and healthy. **Cafeteria** workers cook and serve meals. They make sure that the food is prepared and stored properly.

A counselor can help students who are
having trouble.

Custodians clean hallways and classrooms. They keep the school looking nice.

A **counselor** takes care of students who need extra help. This worker spends time with students who are worried or sad or angry. Sometimes the counselor can offer advice if kids are having a hard time. All of these workers are there to help students just like you!

Helping friends sound out new words is a great way to practice teaching.

Do You Want to Work in a School?

Would you like to work in a school when you grow up? You can start getting ready now. Ask school workers lots of questions. What do they like best about their jobs? What did they have to learn to be able to do their jobs?

Most teachers are good at helping people learn. Do you think you can help

Everyone works together in a school to help students learn.

people learn? Practice by teaching some-
one a simple lesson. Maybe you can help
a friend who is having trouble learning
something. Find ways to share what
you know.

A school can be a great place to work.
Learn as much as you can now. It will help
you decide if a school job is right for you!

Create!

Make a list of things you know that you can share with
others. Can you teach your family the exercises you
do in gym class? Maybe you can tell them about your
history lesson. Check off items on your list as you share
all that you know.

GLOSSARY

assignments (uh-SINE-muhnts) work that is given to a student who must complete it

cafeteria (kaf-uh-TIHR-ee-uh) a lunchroom or area in a school where people gather to eat

counselor (KAUN-seh-luhr) a school worker who gives students advice and guidance

custodians (kuhs-TOE-dee-uhnz) workers who are in charge of cleaning and taking care of a school

librarian (lye-BRER-ee-uhn) workers who are in charge of the books and other materials in a library and help people find what they need

principal (PRIN-suh-pul) a worker who is in charge of a school and makes sure everyone else does a good job and follows the rules

secretary (SEH-kreh-tare-ee) a worker who helps the principal keep the school organized and often handles letters, e-mails, and phone calls

FIND OUT MORE

BOOKS

Lowenstein, Felicia. *What Does a Teacher Do?* Berkeley Heights, N.J.: Enslow Elementary, 2006.

Nelson, Robin, and Stephen G. Donaldson (photographer). *Custodians*. Minneapolis: Lerner Publications Company, 2005.

WEB SITES

KidsHealth— School Counselors

www.kidshealth.org/kid/ feel_better/people/ school_counselors.html
Read about school counselors and how they can help students

U.S. Department of Labor—Bureau of Labor Statistics (Teacher)

www.bls.gov/k12/help01.htm
Learn more about teaching and how you can prepare to be a teacher

INDEX

ABOUT THE AUTHOR

Katie Marsico is the author of more than 30 children's books. She lives in Elmhurst, Illinois, with her husband and two children. She would especially like to thank her cousin, Tracy Bratzke. Tracy is a teacher and helped her research this title.